Probability

by Erin Sullivan

Table of Contents

S0-APO-583

What Is Probability?

Think about the math word **probability**. Does it make you think of the word "probably"? You can use the word "probably" in sentences such as these:

"That cat will probably drink the milk."
"It will probably be warm this summer."

In both sentences, you are describing things that are **likely** to happen.

Probability is a kind of math people do to find out if an event is likely to occur. They use information from the past to predict the future.

Probability can help you answer common questions such as these:

- Will it rain tomorrow?

- Will my favorite baseball player hit a home run?

- What will they serve for lunch today in the cafeteria?

How Can You Use Probability to Predict the Future?

Think about what your school cafeteria serves for lunch. Let's say it's only spaghetti, burgers, hot dogs, and burritos.

This means it's **impossible** that you will have pizza tomorrow. But it's **possible** that you'll have spaghetti tomorrow.

And if you've already had burgers, hot dogs, and burritos this week, then it's likely that you will have spaghetti.

If the cafeteria sends home a note saying, "We're having spaghetti tomorrow no matter what," then it's **certain** you'll be eating spaghetti!

Look at the list below. See if you can decide whether each event is impossible, possible, likely, or certain.

Event	Impossible	Possible	Likely	Certain
Babies will be born tomorrow.				
You will be 8 feet tall.				
The sun will rise.				
Someone will be absent this week.				
You will listen to the radio.				

People also use probability to predict the weather. Scientists who study the weather are called **meteorologists**. They gather **data**, or information, about the weather in their area. They use that data to predict what will probably happen.

Weather Folklore

People have always tried to predict the weather! Here are some old-fashioned predictions. Do you think they might be accurate?

- If the weather in November is warm, then winter will be cold.

- For every fog in August, there will be a snowfall in winter.

- If anthills are high in July, winter will be snowy.

▲ These meteorologists are studying cloud cover over the United States mainland to get a more precise weather forecast.

Here is a weather table for a typical week in February in Los Angeles, California.

Weather Table: February 2–8	
Monday	partly sunny, 65–68 degrees
Tuesday	mostly cloudy, 62 degrees
Wednesday	rainy, 60 degrees
Thursday	rainy, 60 degrees
Friday	partly sunny, 64–69 degrees
Saturday	sunny, 70–75 degrees
Sunday	sunny, 70–75 degrees

Use this data to predict whether the following conditions are impossible, possible, likely, or certain for another February day in Los Angeles.

Weather	Impossible	Possible	Likely	Certain
a rainy day				
a sunny day				
a snowy day				
a day below 30 degrees				
a day above 60 degrees				

How Can You Use Probability to Predict a Winner?

Probability is also an important part of most games. If you play basketball during recess, you make sure that there is an equal number of players on each team. If you play cards, you make sure that each player gets the same number of cards. Two runners in a race will make sure that they are running over the same distance.

When a game is **fair**, both sides have an equal chance of winning. If a game is **unfair**, then one side has a better chance to win than the other.

Teams A and B are having a playoff. Does each team have an equal chance of winning? Why or why not?

Teams C and D are playing a soccer match. Is the game fair? Who is more likely to win? Why?

Have you ever played a game with spinners? You can use probability to predict the result of spinner games, too.

Sophie, Bill, and Tracy are playing a spinner game. If the spinner lands on red, Sophie wins a point. If the spinner lands on blue, Bill wins a point. If the spinner lands on yellow, Tracy wins a point.

If the spinner looks like this, who is most likely to win a point?

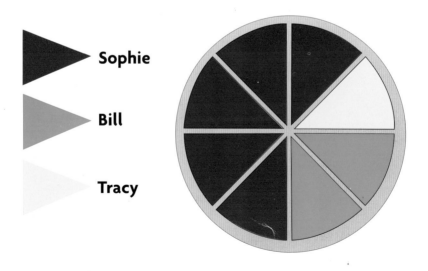

Sophie

Bill

Tracy

Sophie will probably win because five of the eight sections of the spinner are red. Only two of the eight are blue and one of the eight is yellow. You could describe each player's chances of winning like this:

Sophie's probability of winning is $5/8$.

Bill's probability of winning is $2/8$.

Tracy's probability of winning is $1/8$.

What would happen if the same people played the same game with the spinners below? How would their chances of winning change?

Spinner A

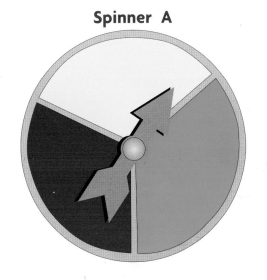

Spinner B

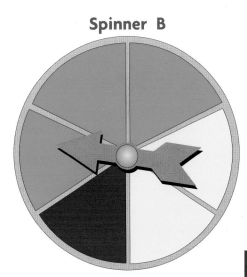

How Can You Use Probability to Predict an Outcome?

You can also use probability when you flip a coin.

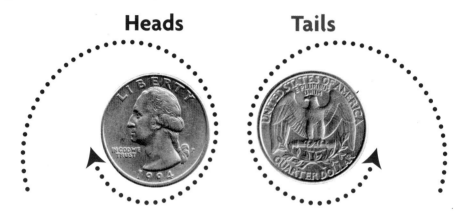

Heads   **Tails**

There are two possible **outcomes** when you flip a coin. You could get heads or you could get tails.

Out of two possible outcomes, your chances of getting heads is 1 out of 2, or $\frac{1}{2}$. There is also a 1 out of 2 chance that you will get tails. So the probability of getting tails is $\frac{1}{2}$ also.

Look at this chart. How many times did Emily flip the coin? What fraction of the time did she get heads? What fraction of the time did she get tails? What is the probability that she will get heads on the next flip?

Emily's Coin Toss Experiment		
TOSS NUMBER	HEADS	TAILS
1	X	
2		X
3		X
4		X
5	X	
6		X
7	X	

Many games use number cubes—and players hope that they will roll the right number at the right time!

Each of the six **faces** of the cube has a number from 1 to 6 on it. How many possible outcomes are there? What is the probability of rolling a 4?

Now imagine that you are rolling two number cubes and adding the digits on the top face of each cube. What are the possible **sums**, or answers?

The lowest possible sum would be 2, if you rolled 1 and 1. The highest sum would be 12, if you rolled 6 and 6. You can also get the same sum by rolling different combinations of numbers. For example, to get 5, you could roll 1 and 4, or 2 and 3.

1 1 = 2   **1 4 = 5**

6 6 = 12   **2 3 = 5**

If you rolled a pair of number cubes 25 times, which sum do you think you would get most often? See for yourself!

Number Cube Experiment

Every time you roll a sum, put a tally mark in the column that has the number that you rolled.

Rolls	SUMS										
	2	3	4	5	6	7	8	9	10	11	12
1											
2											

Look at these gumballs. How many are there altogether?

- How many blue? ⬤
- How many red? ⬤
- How many green? ⬤
- How many yellow? ⬤
- How many white? ◯

Imagine that you close your eyes and pick 1 of the gumballs. What is the probability of your picking a blue one?

There are 15 possible gumballs to pick, or 15 possible outcomes. Of the gumballs, 5 are blue. So there is a 5 out of 15, or $^5/_{15}$, chance that you will pick a blue gumball.

What is the probability of picking each of the other colors? What is the probability of picking a brown gumball?

Students	Girl or Boy?	Hair Color	Glasses?
Bill	boy	blond	no
Maria	girl	brown	no
Colleen	girl	red	no
Pam	girl	black	yes
Tony	boy	brown	no
Kevin	boy	black	no
Sara	girl	blond	no
Tom	boy	brown	no
Darrell	boy	black	yes
Donna	girl	brown	yes

Here is a chart that gives you some information about ten different students. Imagine that you have to walk into their classroom, close your eyes, and tap one person on the shoulder. What is the probability of picking a girl? What is the probability of picking someone who has brown hair? What is the probability of picking someone who wears glasses?

Can you come up with some probability questions to ask about the kids in your own class?

Probability Answers

Page 5

Babies will be born
tomorrow: certain
You will be 8 feet tall: impossible
The sun will rise: certain
Someone will be absent this
week: likely
You will listen to the
radio: possible

Page 7

A rainy day: possible
A sunny day: likely
A snowy day: impossible
A day below 30 degrees: impossible
A day above 60 degrees: likely

Page 9

No. One basket is higher than the
other. The player with the lower
basket is more likely to win.

No. The player with the bigger
goal is more likely to win.

Page 11

Spinner A: Sophie, $1/3$; Bill, $1/3$;
Tracy, $1/3$
Spinner B: Sophie, $1/6$; Bill, $3/6$
or $1/2$; Tracy, $2/6$ or $1/3$

Page 12

There are 2 possible outcomes.
Probability of getting heads is $1/2$.

Page 13

Emily tossed the coin 7 times;
$3/7$ heads, $4/7$ tails; the
probability of getting heads
on the next flip is $1/2$

Page 14

There are 6 possible outcomes.
Probability of rolling a 4 is $1/6$.

Page 15

The sum of 7 will come up
most often because the most
possible combinations add up to 7:
1 + 6, 2 + 5, 3 + 4, 4 + 3,
5 + 2, and 6 + 1

Pages 16–17

5 blue, 4 red, 3 green, 2 yellow,
1 white
Probabilities: $5/15$ for blue, $4/15$
for red, $3/15$ for green, $2/15$ for
yellow, $1/15$ for white, $0/15$ for
brown

Page 18

The probability of picking a girl is
$5/10$, or $1/2$. It is the number of
girls divided by the total number
of students. The probability of
picking someone who has brown
hair is $4/10$; someone who wears
glasses $3/10$.

Glossary

certain   (SER-tun): definitely will happen

data   (DAY-tuh): information

face   (FASE): one side of a number cube

fair   (FAIR): when both sides have an equal chance

impossible   (im-PAH-sih-bul): definitely could not happen

likely   (LY-klee): probably will happen

meteorologists   (mee-tee-uh-RAH-luh-jists): scientists who predict the weather

outcomes   (OWT-kumz): events that happen

possible   (PAH-sih-bul): could happen

probability   (prah-buh-BIH-lih-tee): finding the chances that a certain event will happen

sum   (SUM): the answer to an addition problem

unfair   (un-FAIR): when one side has a better chance than the other

Index